The Low FODMAP Diet

Slow Cooker Cookbook

Table of Contents

Introduction

Do you suffer from horrible gas, bloating and abdominal cramps? What about diarrhea or constipation? If you have any of these digestive issues, you might be suffering from Irritable Bowel Syndrome (IBS). This commonly misdiagnosed condition affects about 1 in 5 Americans, and although there are some medical treatments available, they usually only work to reduce your symptoms—they do not cure the condition. That's why the most effective long-term treatment for IBS involves making changes to your diet.

The Low FODMAP Diet was specifically developed for IBS sufferers and it may be just what you need to relieve your IBS symptoms. This diet is focused on easy-to-digest foods and it excludes the four different types of short-chain carbohydrates called FODMAPs. These include oligosaccharides, polyols, fructose, and lactose. By reducing your consumption of these food groups you can drastically reduce your IBS symptoms and start healing your digestive system. In order to follow this diet you need to avoid high-lactose dairy products, high-fructose fruits, gluten-containing grains, and various natural and artificial sweeteners. Basically, you should be focusing your diet on leafy greens, gluten-free grains, lean meat and eggs, fish and seafood, low-fructose fruits, nuts and seeds, and non-dairy milk.

In switching to the Low FODMAP Diet you may experience a reduction in your IBS symptoms more quickly than you imagined. The longer you stick to the diet, the better your results will be. So, if you are ready to tackle your IBS with the Low FODMAP Diet then simply pick a recipe from this book and get cooking! What do you have to lose?

If the Low FODMAP Diet is a new concept for you, I highly recommend reading The Low FODMAP Diet: 30-Recipe Cookbook and 14-Day Meal Plan For Overcoming IBS For Good. This first book in the series covers all of the information you need to know to in order to implement the Low FODMAP Diet in your lifestyle, both in and out of the slow cooker. It also provides a handy 14-day meal plan in order to get you started and feeling healthy again!

Enjoy!

Low FODMAP Slow Cooker Recipes

BREAKFAST RECIPES

Bacon and Veggie Breakfast Casserole

Servings: 6 to 8

Ingredients:
- 1 lbs. turkey bacon, chopped
- 2 lbs. Russet potatoes, peeled and shredded
- 1 small green pepper, cored and diced
- 1 small carrot, peeled and diced
- 1 cup diced zucchini
- 12 large eggs, beaten well
- 1 cup unsweetened almond milk
- Salt and pepper to taste

Instructions:

1. Heat the bacon in a medium skillet over medium-high heat until it is crisp.
2. Remove the bacon to paper towels to drain.
3. Spread half of the shredded potatoes along the bottom of the slow cooker and top with half the crumbled bacon.
4. Sprinkle on about half of the green peppers, carrots and zucchini.
5. Add the rest of the shredded potatoes and bacon as well as the remaining veggies.
6. Beat together the eggs and almond milk in a bowl then pour it into the slow cooker.
7. Season with salt and pepper to taste then cover and cook for 8 hours on low heat until the casserole is set.

Maple Walnut Oatmeal

Servings: 4

Ingredients:
- 1 ½ cups unsweetened almond milk
- 1 ½ cups water
- 3 cups chopped banana
- 1 cup steel-cut oats, uncooked
- 2 tablespoons coconut sugar
- 1 ½ tablespoons melted coconut oil
- ½ teaspoon ground cinnamon
- Pinch salt
- 4 to 5 tablespoons pure maple syrup
- 1/3 cup chopped walnuts

Instructions:

1. Combine the milk and water in a large saucepan and bring to a boil.
2. Lightly spray the inside of your slow cooker with cooking spray.
3. Pour the heated milk into the slow cooker and stir in the banana, oats, coconut sugar, coconut oil, cinnamon and salt.
4. Cover the slow cooker and cook on low heat for 7 hours.
5. Spoon the oats into bowls and drizzle with maple syrup and sprinkle with walnuts to serve.

Spinach, Red Pepper and Ham Frittata

Servings: 6

Ingredients:
- 6 large eggs, beaten well
- ½ cup canned coconut milk
- ¼ cup unsweetened almond milk
- Salt and pepper to taste
- 1 ½ cups fresh baby spinach, packed
- 1 small red pepper, cored and chopped
- 1 cup diced ham

Instructions:

1. Whisk together your eggs, almond milk, coconut milk, salt and pepper in a mixing bowl.
2. Lightly spray the insert of your slow cooker with cooking spray.
3. Spread the spinach, red pepper and ham in the slow cooker.
4. Pour in your egg mixture and stir gently.
5. Cover the slow cooker and cook on high heat for up to 2 hours until the eggs are set.

Creamy Steel-Cut Oats

Servings: 6 to 8

Ingredients:
- 1 (15-ounce) can coconut milk
- 8 cups water
- 1 to 2 tablespoons coconut sugar
- 1 teaspoon vanilla extract
- 2 cups steel-cut oats, uncooked

Instructions:
1. Stir together the coconut milk, water, sugar and vanilla in the slow cooker.
2. Add the oats and stir until well combined.
3. Cover the slow cooker and cook on low heat for 8 hours or overnight.
4. Serve the oats hot topped with fresh fruit, nuts, or seeds.

Cinnamon Breakfast Quinoa

Servings: 5 to 6

Ingredients:
- 3 cups unsweetened almond milk
- 1 cup uncooked quinoa, rinsed well
- 4 large pitted dates, chopped
- ¼ cup hulled sunflower seeds
- 2 teaspoons ground cinnamon
- ½ teaspoon ground nutmeg
- 1 ½ teaspoon vanilla extract
- Pinch salt

Instructions:
1. Stir together the almond milk and quinoa in the slow cooker.
2. Add your dates, sunflower seeds, cinnamon, nutmeg and vanilla.
3. Season with a pinch of salt and stir well.
4. Cover the slow cooker and cook on high heat for 2 hours until tender. Serve hot.

SOUPS AND STEWS

Lamb and Chickpea Stew

Servings: 4 to 6

Ingredients:
- 2 tablespoons olive oil
- 2 ½ lbs. boneless lamb shoulder, cut into chunks
- Salt and pepper to taste
- 1 tablespoon fresh grated ginger
- 3 teaspoons ground cumin
- 2 teaspoon dried coriander
- ½ teaspoon ground cinnamon
- 1 (14-ounce) can diced tomatoes
- 1 ½ cups chicken broth
- 1 (15-ounce) can chickpeas, rinsed and drained
- 1 cup chopped butternut squash

Instructions:
1. Heat the oil in a large skillet over medium heat.
2. Season the lamb with salt and pepper to taste and add it to the skillet.
3. Cook for 3 to 4 minutes on each side until browned then transfer to the slow cooker.
4. Stir the spices into the skillet and cook for 2 minutes.
5. Add the tomatoes and chicken broth then stir well and bring to a boil.
6. Transfer the mixture to the slow cooker and stir in the chickpeas and butternut squash.
7. Cover and cook on low heat for 5 to 6 hours until tender.

Beefy Vegetable Curry

Servings: 4 to 6

Ingredients:
- 3 lbs. beef stew meat, chopped
- 1 lbs. small red potatoes, chopped
- 2 tablespoons curry powder
- 1 tablespoon fresh grated ginger
- 1 teaspoon ground cumin
- Salt and pepper to taste
- 2 (14.5-ounce) cans roasted diced tomatoes
- Fresh chopped cilantro

Instructions:

1. Place the beef and potatoes in a zippered freezer bag.
2. Combine the curry powder, ginger, cumin, salt and pepper in a small bowl then add to the bag.
3. Toss to coat then spread the mixture in the slow cooker.
4. Pour in the tomatoes then cover and cook for 7 hours on low heat.
5. Uncover the slow cooker and let stand for 10 minutes then serve with fresh cilantro.

Hearty Lentil Stew

Servings: 8 to 10

Ingredients:
- 2 cups uncooked lentils, rinsed well
- 3 cups beef broth
- 1 cup water
- 2 large carrots, peeled and diced
- 1 large stalk celery, sliced
- 1 large red potato, peeled and chopped
- 2 (14-ounce) cans diced tomatoes, drained
- 1 large bay leaf
- ½ teaspoon ground coriander
- ¼ teaspoon crushed red pepper
- Pinch ground turmeric
- Salt and pepper to taste

Instructions:
1. Combine the lentils, beef broth and water in the slow cooker – stir well.
2. Stir in the carrots, celery and potato as well as the canned tomatoes.
3. Add the remaining ingredients and stir until well combined.
4. Cover the slow cooker and cook for 5 to 6 hours on low until tender.

Slow Cooker Pumpkin Soup

Servings: 8 to 10

Ingredients:
- 1 medium-sized pie pumpkin, peeled, seeded and chopped
- 2 large Yukon gold potatoes, peeled and chopped
- 3 cups vegetable stock
- 1 ½ teaspoons curry powder
- Salt and pepper to taste
- 1 cup canned coconut milk

Instructions:

1. Toss together the pumpkin, potatoes, vegetable stock and curry powder in the slow cooker.
2. Season with salt and pepper to taste.
3. Cover and cook on low heat for 6 to 8 hours until the vegetables are tender.
4. Turn off the heat and puree the soup using an immersion blender.
5. Whisk in the coconut milk then serve hot.

Beef Bourguignon Stew

Servings: 6 to 8

Ingredients:
- 1 cup beef broth
- 2 cups dry red wine
- 2 tablespoons almond flour
- 3 lbs. boneless beef chuck roast, chopped into cubes
- 4 large carrots, peeled and chopped
- 2 large Yukon gold potatoes, peeled and chopped
- 2 large stalks celery, peeled and chopped
- Salt and pepper to taste
- 1 large bay leaf
- 4 sprigs fresh thyme

Instructions:

1. Whisk together the beef stock, wine and flour in a bowl.
2. Toss together the beef and vegetables in the slow cooker.
3. Season with salt and pepper to taste.
4. Add the bay leaf and thyme then pour in the beef stock mixture.
5. Cover the slow cooker and cook on low heat for 6 to 8 hours until the beef is tender.
6. Discard the bay leaf and thyme and serve the stew hot.

SIDE DISHES

Southwest-Style Quinoa

Servings: 4 to 6

Ingredients:
- 1 cup uncooked quinoa, rinsed well
- 1 cup frozen corn, thawed
- 1 (14-ounce) can chickpeas, rinsed and drained
- 1 large red pepper, cored and chopped
- 1 cup diced tomatoes
- 2 teaspoons ground cumin
- Salt and pepper to taste
- 1 ½ tablespoons adobo sauce (from canned chilies in adobo sauce)
- 2 cups vegetable broth

Instructions:
1. Lightly grease the insert of your slow cooker with cooking spray.
2. Stir together your quinoa, corn and chickpeas in the slow cooker.
3. Add your red pepper, tomatoes, cumin, salt and pepper as well as the adobo sauce.
4. Stir in the vegetable broth then cover the slow cooker.
5. Cook on high heat for 3 to 4 hours until the quinoa is tender.

Sweet Potato Gratin

Servings: 10 to 12

Ingredients:
- 3 large sweet potato, peeled and sliced thin
- 1 tablespoon blanched almond flour
- ½ teaspoon dried thyme
- Salt and pepper to taste
- ¼ cup nutritional yeast
- ½ cup vegetable broth

Instructions:
1. Lightly grease the insert of your slow cooker with cooking spray.
2. Stir together the sweet potato, almond flour, thyme, salt and pepper in the slow cooker.
3. Add the nutritional yeast then stir in the vegetable broth then cover the slow cooker.
4. Cook on low heat for 4 hours or until the sweet potato is tender.

Maple Orange-Glazed Carrots

Servings: 5 to 6

Ingredients:

- 1 lbs. carrots, peeled and sliced
- 2 tablespoons melted coconut oil
- 2 to 3 tablespoons pure maple syrup
- Salt and pepper to taste

Instructions:

1. Lightly grease the insert of your slow cooker with cooking spray.
2. Spread your carrots in the slow cooker and toss with the coconut oil.
3. Drizzle the maple syrup over the carrots and season with salt and pepper to taste.
4. Cover the slow cooker and cook on high heat for 3 hours until tender.

Creamy Slow Cooker Polenta

Servings: 4

Ingredients:
- 1 cup unsweetened almond milk
- 1 cup canned coconut milk
- 1/3 cup coarse-grain polenta
- Salt to taste
- 2 tablespoons coconut oil

Instructions:
1. Lightly grease the insert of your slow cooker with cooking spray.
2. Heat the almond and coconut milks in a saucepan over medium-high heat.
3. Stir in the polenta then season with salt.
4. Boil for about 2 to 3 minutes then pour the whole mixture into the slow cooker.
5. Cover and cook on high heat for 2 hours, stirring every 30 minutes.
6. Uncover the slow cooker and stir in the coconut oil before serving.

Herbed Root Vegetables

Servings: 8 to 10

Ingredients:
- 4 large carrots, peeled and chopped
- 2 large sweet potatoes, peeled and chopped
- 2 large parsnips, peeled and chopped
- 2 large turnips, peeled and chopped
- 2 to 3 tablespoons pure maple syrup
- 1 tablespoon melted coconut oil
- 2 teaspoons fresh chopped rosemary
- 2 teaspoons fresh chopped thyme
- Salt and pepper to taste

Instructions:
1. Lightly grease the insert of your slow cooker with cooking spray.
2. Combine the vegetables in the slow cooker.
3. Whisk together the maple syrup, oil, rosemary, thyme, salt and pepper in a bowl.
4. Pour the mixture into the slow cooker and stir well.
5. Cover the slow cooker and cook on low heat for 4 to 5 hours until tender.

ENTREES

Easy Chicken Cacciatore

Servings: 6 to 8

Ingredients:
- 1 tablespoon olive oil
- 4 pounds bone-in chicken thighs and drumsticks
- Salt and pepper to taste
- 1 large red pepper, cored and sliced
- 1 large green pepper, cored and sliced
- 2 (14-ounce) cans crushed tomatoes in juice
- ½ cup cooking sherry
- 5 tablespoons almond flour
- 2 tablespoons fresh chopped oregano
- 1 ½ tablespoons fresh chopped thyme
- 1 tablespoon fresh chopped basil

Instructions:
1. Lightly grease the insert of your slow cooker with cooking spray.
2. Heat a large skillet over medium-high heat with the oil.
3. Season the chicken with salt and pepper to taste and add it to the skillet.
4. Cook for 4 to 5 minutes on each side until browned then transfer to the slow cooker.
5. Add the red peppers and green peppers to the slow cooker.
6. In a mixing bowl, stir together the tomatoes, sherry, flour, and spices.
7. Pour the tomato mixture into the slow cooker and cover it.
8. Cook for 3 hours on low heat until the chicken is cooked through.

Slow Cooker Pulled Pork

Servings: 6 to 8

Ingredients:
- 4 to 4 ½ lbs. boneless pork shoulder
- 3 teaspoons ground cumin
- ½ tablespoon chili powder
- Salt and pepper to taste

Instructions:
1. Lightly grease the insert of your slow cooker with cooking spray.
2. Rub the pork with the cumin and chili powder then season with salt and pepper to taste.
3. Place the pork in the slow cooker and cover it.
4. Cook on low heat for 8 hours until the meat starts to fall off the bone.
5. Remove the pork to a cutting board and shred the meat with two forks. Serve hot.

Lamb Shanks with Cranberry Sauce

Servings: 4 to 6

Ingredients:
- 2 tablespoons olive oil
- 6 lamb shanks, bone-in
- Salt and pepper to taste
- 1 ½ cups chicken stock
- 1 cup dry red wine
- 1 (14-ounce) can whole cranberry sauce
- 3 tablespoons fresh chopped rosemary

Instructions:
1. Lightly grease the insert of your slow cooker with cooking spray.
2. Heat the oil in a large skillet over medium-high heat.
3. Season the lamb shanks with salt and pepper to taste then add them to the skillet.

4. Cook for 3 to 4 minutes on each side until browned then transfer to the slow cooker.
5. Whisk together the chicken stock, red wine, and cranberry sauce in a bowl.
6. Stir in the rosemary and season with salt and pepper to taste.
7. Pour the mixture over the lamb in the slow cooker.
8. Cover and cook for 6 to 7 hours on high until the lamb is cooked through.

Chicken Tikka Masala

Servings: 6 to 8

Ingredients:
- 2 ½ lbs. boneless chicken thighs, chopped
- 2 (14-ounce) cans crushed tomatoes in juice
- 2/3 cups tikka masala paste
- 1 bunch fresh chopped cilantro

Instructions:
1. Lightly grease the insert of your slow cooker with cooking spray.
2. Combine the chicken, tomatoes and tikka masala paste in the slow cooker.
3. Cover and cook on high heat for 3 to 3 ½ hours.
4. Sprinkle the mixture with chopped cilantro and serve with steamed white rice.

Homemade Beef Pot Roast

Servings: 6 to 8

Ingredients:
- 2 lbs. boneless beef chuck roast, halved
- ¼ cup soy sauce
- 2 lbs. carrots, peeled and sliced
- 2 lbs. red potatoes, halved
- 1 tablespoon olive oil
- Salt and pepper to taste
- 3 tablespoons tomato paste

Instructions:
1. Lightly grease the insert of your slow cooker with cooking spray.
2. Place the chuck roast in a zippered freezer bag and add the soy sauce.
3. Toss to coat then marinate in the fridge overnight or for 8 hours.
4. Place the carrots and potatoes in the slow cooker.

5. Heat the oil in a large skillet over medium-high heat.
6. Season the roast with salt and pepper to taste and add it to the skillet.
7. Cook for 4 to 5 minutes on each side until evenly browned.
8. Transfer the roast to the slow cooker then stir the tomato paste into the skillet.
9. Pour the tomato paste over the roast and cover the slow cooker.
10. Cook on high heat for 1 hour then reduce to low and cook for 8 hours until tender.

DESSERTS

Maple Poached Pears

Servings: 6

Ingredients:
- 6 medium ripe pears
- 2 cups unsweetened cranberry juice
- ½ cup organic cane sugar
- 1/3 cup fresh squeezed orange juice
- ¼ cup pure maple syrup
- 1 tablespoon vanilla extract
- 2 teaspoons ground cinnamon

Instructions:
1. Peel the pears and use a melon baller to remove the cores from the bottom.
2. Whisk together the cranberry juice, sugar, orange juice and maple syrup in the slow cooker.

3. Stir in the vanilla and cinnamon then place the pears in the slow cooker, standing them upright.
4. Cover the slow cooker and cook on high heat for 3 hours until the pears are tender.

Pineapple Bananas Foster

Servings: 6 to 8

Ingredients:
- ½ cup brown sugar, packed
- 3 tablespoons coconut oil
- 4 tablespoons canned coconut milk
- 4 tablespoons dark rum
- 4 medium bananas, peeled and sliced
- 1 cup fresh chopped pineapple
- ½ teaspoon ground cinnamon

Instructions:
1. Lightly grease the insert of the slow cooker with cooking spray.
2. Stir together the brown sugar, coconut oil, coconut milk and rum in the slow cooker.
3. Cover the slow cooker and cook on low heat for 1 hour.

4. Stir the mixture well then stir in the pineapple, banana, and cinnamon.
5. Cover and cook on low heat for about 15 minutes until the fruit is tender.

Cinnamon Raisin Rice Pudding

Servings: 8 to 10

Ingredients:
- 7 cups unsweetened almond milk, divided
- 2 cups long-grain rice
- ¾ cups organic cane sugar
- Pinch salt
- 1 cup seedless raisins
- 1 teaspoon ground cinnamon
- 1 teaspoon vanilla extract

Instructions:
1. Lightly grease the insert of your slow cooker with cooking spray.
2. Stir together 6 cups of almond milk along with the rice, sugar and salt in the slow cooker.

3. Cover the slow cooker and cook on high heat for 3 ½ to 4 hours until creamy.
4. Stir in the rest of the almond milk along with the raisins, cinnamon and vanilla extract.
5. Spoon the rice pudding into bowls to serve.

Tropical Tapioca Pudding

Servings: 8 to 10

Ingredients:
- 2 (14-ounce) cans coconut milk
- ¾ cup organic cane sugar
- ½ cup pearl tapioca
- 1 large egg, beaten well
- 1/3 cup diced pineapple
- 1/3 cup diced papaya
- ½ cup unsweetened shredded coconut

Instructions:
1. Lightly grease the insert of your slow cooker with cooking spray.
2. Stir together the coconut milk, sugar and tapioca in the slow cooker.
3. Cover and cook on low heat for about 2 hours.

4. Beat the egg in a small bowl then beat in about ½ cup of the tapioca mixture.
5. Stir the egg mixture back into the slow cooker then cover and cook for another 30 minutes on low heat.
6. Turn off the heat and stir in the pineapple, papaya, and coconut. Serve warm.

Strawberry Oatmeal Crisp

Servings: 6 to 8

Ingredients:
- 1 lbs. frozen sliced strawberries (or fresh)
- 1 ¼ cups quick-cooking oats
- ½ cup blanched almond flour
- ½ cup chopped pecans or almonds
- 2 teaspoons ground cinnamon
- Pinch salt
- ¼ cup pure maple syrup
- ¼ cup coconut oil, room temperature

Instructions:
1. Lightly grease the insert of your slow cooker with cooking spray.
2. Spread the strawberries on the bottom of the slow cooker.

3. Combine the oats, almond flour, pecans, cinnamon and salt in a bowl.
4. Stir in the maple syrup and coconut oil until it forms a crumbled mixture.
5. Spread the oat mixture over the strawberries.
6. Cover the slow cooker and cook on low heat for 4 to 5 hours until bubbling.

SAUCES AND SPREADS

Meaty Beef Ragu Sauce

Servings: yields about 6 pints

Ingredients:
- 1 tablespoon olive oil
- 2 lbs. lean ground beef
- 2 large red peppers, cored and chopped
- 3 (14-ounce) cans diced tomatoes with juice
- 2 (14.5-ounce) cans tomato sauce
- 1 (6-oucne) can tomato paste
- ¼ cup fresh chopped basil
- 1 tablespoon organic cane sugar
- 1 teaspoon dried oregano
- Salt and pepper to taste

Instructions:

1. Lightly grease the insert of your slow cooker with cooking spray.
2. Heat the oil in a large skillet over medium heat.
3. Add the beef and red peppers – cook for 8 to 10 minutes until the beef is cooked through.
4. Transfer the mixture to the slow cooker and stir in the remaining ingredients.
5. Cover the slow cooker and cook on low heat for 8 to 9 hours.

Spiced Pumpkin Butter Spread

Servings: yields 4 pints

Ingredients:

- 1 (15-ounce) can pumpkin puree
- 1 ¼ cups organic cane sugar
- ¾ cups brown sugar, packed
- 1 ¼ teaspoon ground cinnamon
- ½ teaspoon ground nutmeg
- ¼ teaspoon ground ginger
- Pinch ground cloves

Instructions:

1. Stir together the pumpkin, sugar and brown sugar in a slow cooker.
2. Add the remaining ingredients and stir until well combined.
3. Cover the slow cooker and cook on high heat for 3 hours, stirring occasionally.
4. Spoon the pumpkin butter into glass pint jars and cover tightly with the lids.

Homemade Barbecue Sauce

Servings:

Ingredients:
- 4 cups organic ketchup
- ½ cup water
- ¼ cup brown sugar, packed
- 2 tablespoons Worcestershire sauce
- 1 to 2 tablespoons molasses
- 1 tablespoon stone-ground mustard
- 3 teaspoons apple cider vinegar
- 3 teaspoons paprika
- 2 teaspoons celery salt
- ½ teaspoon ground black pepper

Instructions:
1. Lightly grease the insert of your slow cooker with cooking spray.

2. Stir together the ketchup, water, brown sugar, molasses and Worcestershire sauce in the slow cooker.
3. Add the remaining ingredients and stir until well combined.
4. Cover the slow cooker and cook on low heat for 6 to 8 hours.
5. Stir the sauce well or puree it using an immersion blender then store in the fridge.

Fruity Blueberry Butter Spread

Servings: yields 3 pints

Ingredients:
- 12 cups fresh blueberries
- 2 cups organic cane sugar
- ½ tablespoon ground cinnamon
- ½ teaspoon ground nutmeg
- 1 large lemon, juiced and zested

Instructions:
1. Place the blueberries in a food processor and blend into a puree.
2. Transfer the blueberry puree to the slow cooker and cook on low heat for 1 hour.
3. Stir the blueberry mixture well then cook on low for another 5 hours with the lid cracked.
4. Add the remaining ingredients and stir well then cook for 1 hour more.
5. Store the blueberry butter spread in glass jars are room temperature.

Easy Marinara Sauce

Servings: yields about 3 pints

Ingredients:
- 4 (14-ounce) cans crushed tomatoes
- 1 (6-ounce) can tomato paste
- 1 ½ tablespoons brown sugar, packed
- 1 tablespoon balsamic vinegar
- 2 large bay leaves
- 3 teaspoons dried oregano
- 3 teaspoon dried basil
- Salt and pepper to taste

Instructions:
1. Combine the tomatoes, tomato paste, brown sugar and balsamic vinegar in the slow cooker.
2. Stir in the remaining ingredients and cover the slow cooker.

3. Cook on low heat for 8 hours then stir well.
4. Remove the bay leaves and season the sauce to taste with salt – puree using an immersion blender, if desired.

Thanks For Reading!

Don't forget to check out *The Low FODMAP Diet Cookbook and 14-Day Meal Plan For Overcoming IBS For Good*, available in paperback and on Kindle!

This first book in the series covers all of the information you need to know to in order to implement the Low FODMAP Diet in your lifestyle, both in and out of the slow cooker. It also provides a handy 14-day meal plan in order to get you started and feeling healthy again!

Enjoy!

Made in the USA
Lexington, KY
31 March 2017